DATE DUE

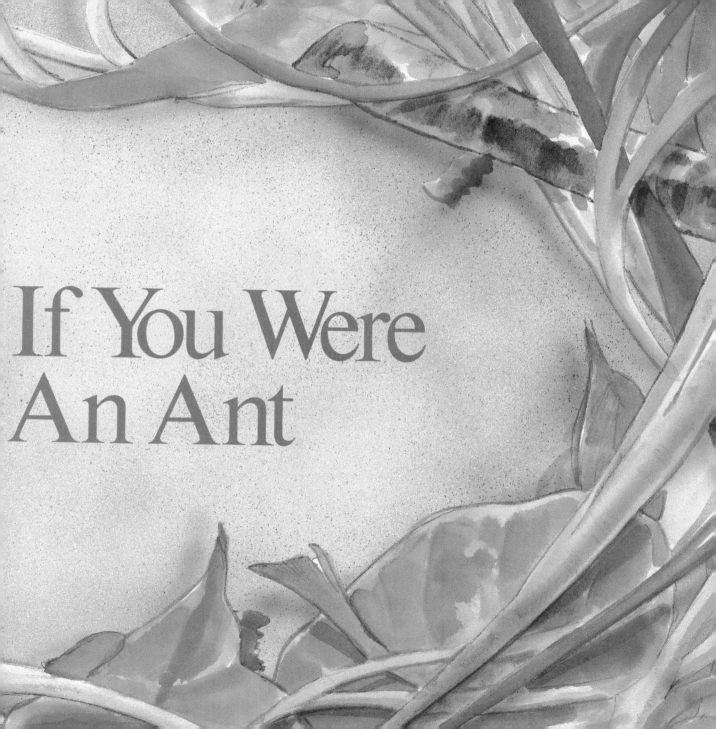

If You Were
An Ant

NOTE TO PARENTS: IF YOU WERE A . . . is told through
the eyes of the animal as a means of providing children
with facts in an engaging and interactive manner.
With each book, children hone their powers of observation
and gain an understanding of the world around them.

Produced by Daniel Weiss Associates, Inc.
27 West 20 Street, New York, NY 10011.

Published by Silver Press, a division of
Silver Burdett Press, Inc., Simon & Schuster, Inc.
Prentice Hall Bldg., Englewood Cliffs, NJ 07632
For information address: Silver Press.

Printed in the United States of America
10 9 8 7 6 5 4 3 2 1

Library of Congress Cataloging-in-Publication Data

Calder, S.J.
If you were an ant / S.J. Calder; illustrations by Cornelius Van Wright.
p. cm.—(First facts)
Summary: An introduction to the physical characteristics, habits
and natural environment of the wood ant.
1. Ants—Juvenile literature. [1. Ants.] I. Van Wright,
Cornelius, ill. II. Title. III. Series: First facts.
(Englewood Cliffs, N.J.)
QL568.F7C28 1989   89-6411
595.79'6—dc20   CIP
                                                    AC
ISBN 0-671-68603-8   ISBN 0-671-68597-X (lib. bdg.)

 **First Facts**™

If You Were An Ant

Written by S. J. Calder
Illustrated by Cornelius Van Wright

Silver Press

Look down on the ground!
Can you see me?

I am an ant—a wood ant.
You can find me in a forest.
I live and work with many other ants
in a colony.

You may have seen me coming
and going from my nest.
I am always very busy. I am a worker.
One of my jobs is to work on my nest.

I gather pieces of twigs and leaves in my jaws.
Then I build an anthill.
Gather and build. Gather and build.
That is how my nest is made.

My nest is dark.
There are many rooms and tunnels
that go deep into the ground.

Does your home have rooms and halls?

Nurseries

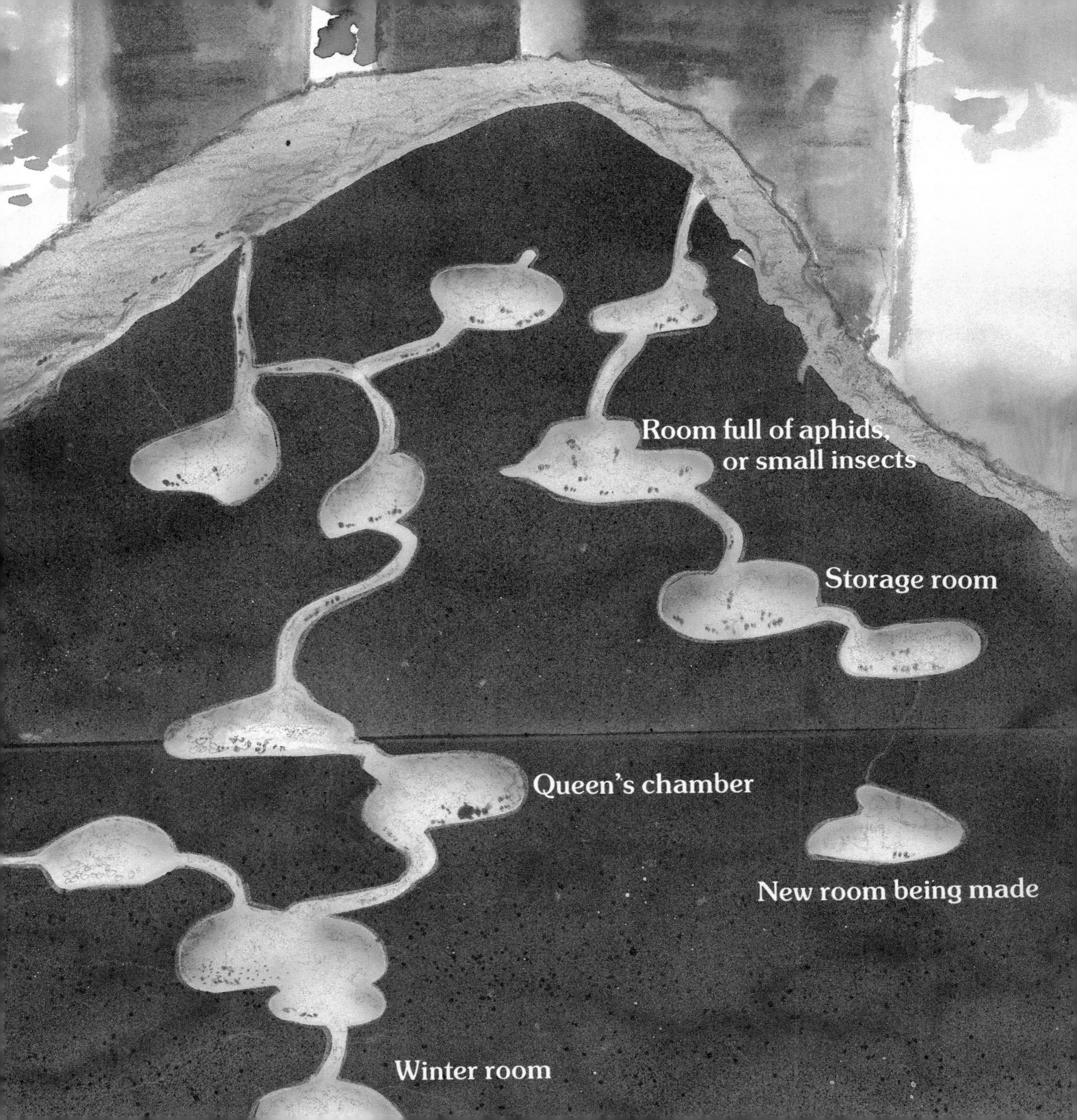

Room full of aphids, or small insects

Storage room

Queen's chamber

New room being made

Winter room

Each nest has one queen.
She is the biggest ant.
Male ants mate with the
queen in the air.
Then they wander off and die.
The queen now goes to the nest
and lays eggs.

I help care for the queen
by feeding and grooming her.

Like all ants, I began as a tiny egg.
Soon, my egg hatched and became a larva . . .
then a pupa.
Soon I was born.

Egg

Larva—a white, wormlike creature

Pupa—a growing ant covered by a thin, see-through skin

Ant

Head

Thorax

Abdomen

Like all insects, my body has three
main parts with a hard shell-like covering.

Look closely at my head.
You will see that I have two antennae.
Each one has smaller parts.
I can move my antennae easily to
smell, touch, taste, and hear.

What do you use to smell, touch, taste, and hear?

I have six legs.
On each leg, I have two hooked claws.
My claws help me to climb trees,
and to walk upside down on branches and leaves.

On my two front legs, I have combs.
I use the combs to rub my other legs
and antennae until they are clean and smooth.

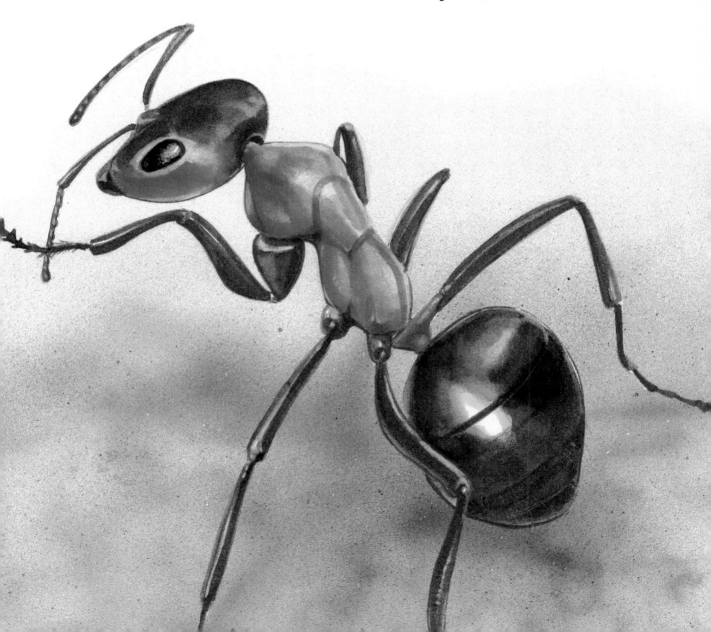

When I am not building my nest,
or caring for the queen,
I hunt for food.

I catch caterpillars, flies,
beetles, and butterflies.
I also drink the sugar drops
from aphids.

When I leave my nest,
I put down a scent trail.
Then I can find my way back easily.
Look at all the other ants on the trail.

I may be small, but I am strong for my size.
I can lift things that are ten times heavier
than I am.
Some ants can lift things fifty times heavier!
If you were that strong, you could pick up a
small elephant!

If something is too big and heavy, other workers help me to carry it.

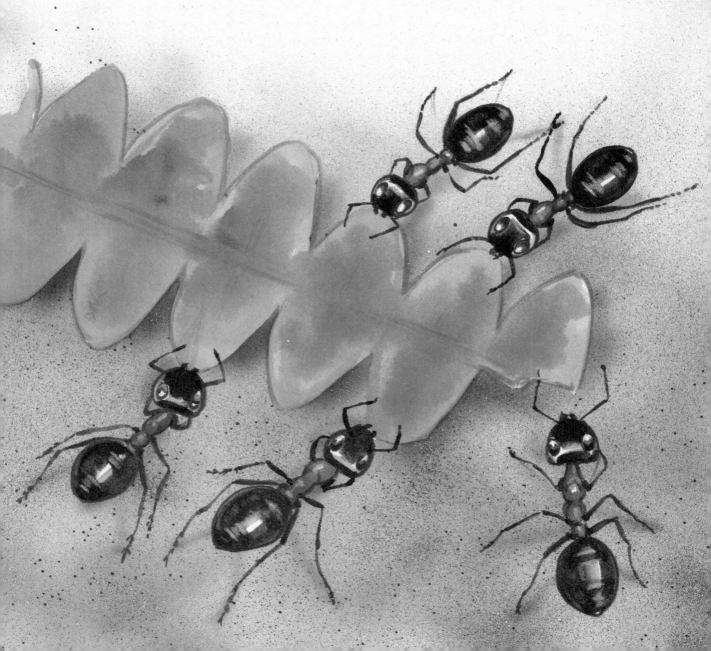

Wait! I smell a warning.
Another ant tells me an enemy is near.
I must be careful as I go.
Here are my enemies:

Spiders

Frogs

Anteaters

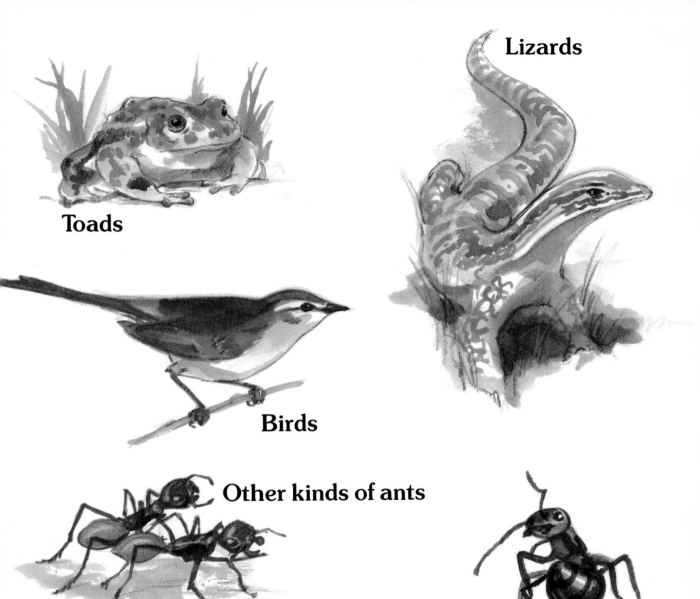

Toads

Lizards

Birds

Other kinds of ants

If I am attacked, I try to protect myself by biting or stinging.

I made it! And I found an aphid.
Now that it is night,
I cannot look for more food.
I am tired, so I will rest.

In winter, when it is cold,
I go down, down, down,
to a warm room at the bottom of the nest.
I stay there until
the weather gets warmer.
Then I come out again.

I am just one of more than 10,000 different kinds of ants.

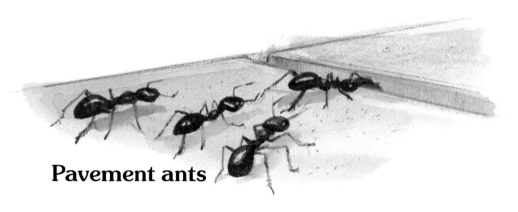

Pavement ants

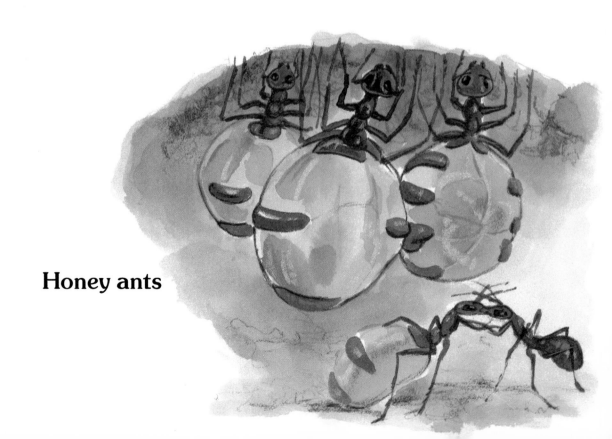

Honey ants

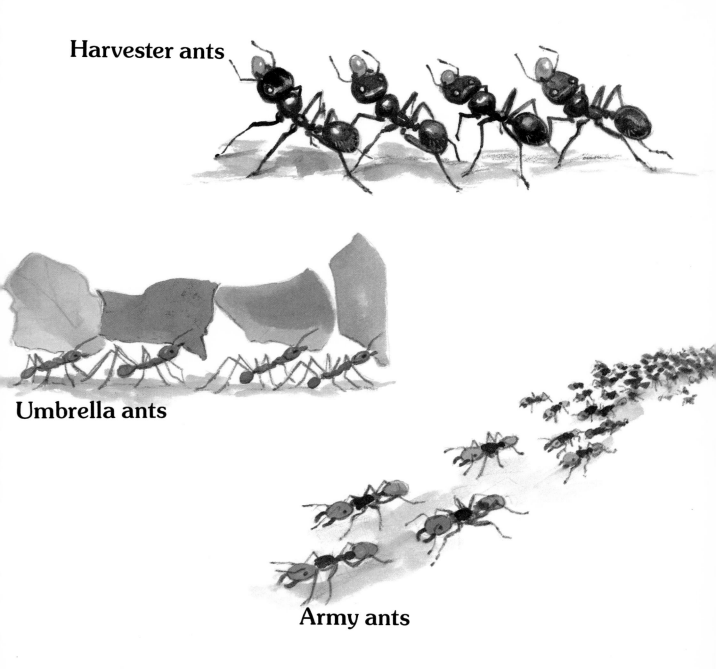

Harvester ants

Umbrella ants

Army ants

To watch ants at work,
make an ant farm. Here's how:

1. Fill a large jar about 3/4 full with soil.
   Add small leaves.

2. Put seeds onto a piece of
   cardboard (outside) to
   attract ants.

3. Carefully drop ants and
   seeds into the jar.

4. Add a small, damp sponge, so the ants will have water.

5. Punch holes in the jar lid, so the ants can breathe.

6. Keep the jar in a dark place until you want to watch them.

Then let the ants go free outdoors!

The next time you are outside,
look for me on the ground.
I will be busy building and hunting.
Work never ends!